William Bolcom

Chalumeau

for Solo Clarinet in B♭

ISBN 978-1-4234-4266-0

EDWARD B. MARKS MUSIC COMPANY

EXCLUSIVELY DISTRIBUTED BY

HAL•LEONARD® CORPORATION

7777 W. BLUEMOUND RD. P.O. BOX 13819 MILWAUKEE, WI 53213

www.ebmarks.com
www.halleonard.com

Chalumeau is a Michigan State University Sesquicentennial Commission, funded by the Office of Research and Graduate Studies and the College of Arts and Letters. It was premiered by Caroline Hartig at the 2005 International ClarinetFest in Tama, Tokyo, Japan on July 20, 2005 in the Recital Hall of Parthenon Tama.

PERFORMANCE NOTES

Accidentals remain in force throughout a beamed group (and in some cases are reiterated even in within a group).

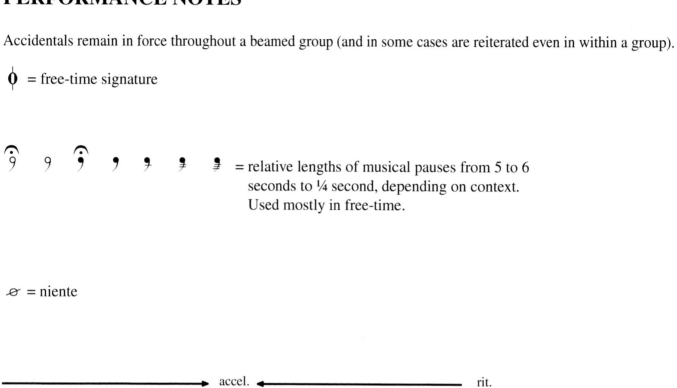

= free-time signature

= relative lengths of musical pauses from 5 to 6 seconds to ¼ second, depending on context. Used mostly in free-time.

= niente

accel.   rit.

For Caroline Hartig

CHALUMEAU

for Solo Clarinet in B♭

WILLIAM BOLCOM
(2004)

Free; *gently moving forward*

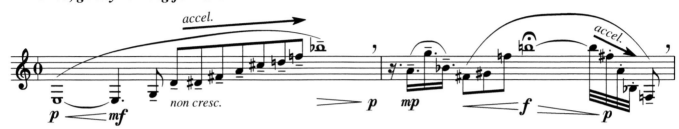

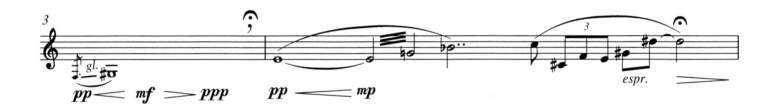

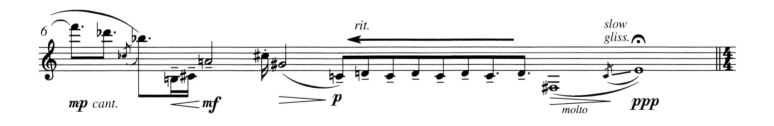

Copyright © 2005 Edward B. Marks Music Company and Bolcom Music
All Rights Reserved   International Copyright Secured

*These metronome markings are relative, approximate, and negotiable.

3

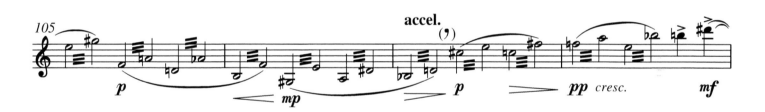

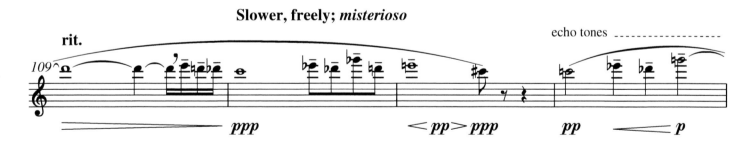

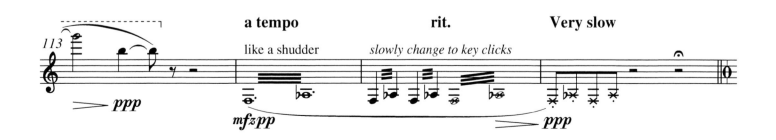